DIEN PIEN PHU

a guide for tourists
by
Richard Baker

ISBN 978-1477518939

Ink & Lens, Ltd

To the people of Vietnam and France and their continued friendship

A Subtle Invasion

No one expected a history professor and his amateur army of Vietnamese peasants to defeat a modern French military force of highly trained professional soldiers, including the famed French Foreign Legion, and officers educated at the finest European military institutes. The world had a surprise coming. The Vietnamese would not be denied their freedom.

The road to Dien Bien Phu is a long one starting with the arrival in Vietnam of Jesuit and Franciscan priests, many from France. The most notable one was Alexandre de Rhodes who arrived in 1627. He learned Vietnamese very quickly and impressed the Trinh emperor in Hanoi. The emperor's advisors were not easily impressed and feared what they viewed as a brutal and domineering religion that would eventually undermine the emperor and the Vietnamese people. De Rhodes was exiled, but not before converting many people and writing a Vietnamese dictionary, using an alphabet of his own invention, that is still used today

Back in France he started the Paris Foreign Missions Society to raise money, gain power and continue to interfere in Vietnam. He managed to return to the country several times. The Trinh family in the north, and the Nguyen family in the south, were fighting a civil war. Rhodes decided to try his luck with the Nguyen faction. His luck was no better with them and he was condemned to death, but was eventually exiled. Back in France he asked King Louis XIV to help spread Christianity to the Far East.

In the 1770's the Nguyen family was overthrown. One member of the family, Nguyen Anh, escaped to the island of Phu Quoc where a priest named Pigneau de Behaine protected him. De Behaine saw an opportunity to monopolize the religions of Vietnam through Christianity. He returned to France to ask the new King, Louis XVI, to help return Nguyen to the throne. He then traveled to India and convinced a number of rich merchants that they could exploit the Vietnamese by establishing a spice trade with them. They agreed to help and eventually Nguyn Anh was restored to his throne. With continued French help, he managed to unify the country calling it Vietnam for the first time and changed his name to Emperor Gai Long.

Emperor Gai Long was happy to use the French to regain control of Vietnam, but he did not trust them or their religion. He said, "The perverse religion of the Europeans corrupts the hearts of men."

The Christians attempted to overthrow the next Emperor, Min Manh, who tried to throw them out of the country. The Christians were growing stronger, however. They started to build their own army to gain power and force the Vietnamese to bow to their God.

When the nsxt emperor, Thieu Tri, continued to oppose Christianity, the French government sent a fleet of warships to Tourane, (later named Da Nang) in central Vietnam, claiming they were there to rescue an imprisoned missionary named Dominique Lefebvre. Although Lefebvre had already been released, the French still decided to shell the town and destroyed the harbor.

Emperor To Duc ascended the throne in 1847 and decided once and for all to drive out the Christians. He realized the only way to eliminate them was to kill the priests. After two were killed, France decided to invade the country and expand their empire.

A dozen French warships, commanded by Admiral Charles Rigault de Genouilly, sailed to Tourane in 1858 after Emperor Louis Napoleon decided to invade Vietnam. De Genouilly had helped destroy Tourane eleven years earlier. With him were over 2,000 soldiers. They had little difficulty securing the city, but there were not enough troops to take over the surrounding countryside. The French were trapped inside the city while the Vietnamese guerrillas controlled the countryside. This pattern remained essentially unchanged right through the defeat of the Americans when Vietnam finally earned her freedom from foreign invaders.

Knowing he could only capture cities, de Genouilly took part of his forces and sailed south to Saigon where much money might be earned from the outlying paddies, rich with rice. The city fell in 1859. Controlling both cities proved too difficult so Tourane was abandoned.

France sent fresh troops to Saigon to help capture much of the surrounding area. Vietnamese Emperor Tu Doc realized he could not defend the country against the superior French forces so he turned over the area around Saigon to them. Vietnamese guerrillas, with a long history of resisting invaders, especially the Chinese, did not agree and they fought the French at every opportunity.

French forces continued to grow and to take more land in the south. They even invaded Cambodia where the weak king quickly surrendered.

Emperor Tu Doc continued to hold Hanoi and the northern part of Vietnam. That soon changeind.

In 1873 a French merchant in Hanoi decided to start his own war. In order to secure and protect his trading interests, Jean Dupuis formed a small army and, with his employees, managed to take over part of the city. He quickly asked the French military to come to his aid. The relief force completed the job of capturing the city and in occupying the surrounding area. Vietnamese guerrillas drove them back into the city. Again Emperor Tu Doc signed a treaty with France agreeing to give them control of southern Vietnam if they would give up the north. France agreed, but not for long.

France knew they needed more troops to control all of Vietnam so they waited patiently in the south as they increased their forces. When they felt strong enough they attacked the north in the county outside of Hanoi. Again determined Vietnamese guerrillas defeated them.

When Emperor Tu Doc died in 1883, Vietnam was left for a short time without a leader and in chaos. France struck again attacking the Vietnamese capital at Hue. Vietnamese government officials agreed to surrender the city but the new Emperor, Ham Nghi, resisted. French general Roussell de Courcy started to destroy the city as Emperor Ham Nghi fled Vietnam leaving the entire country to France.

The French appointed a member of the Vietnamese royal family, Dong Khanh as ruler. France now controlled Vietnam, Cambodia, and soon, Laos in what came to be known as French Indochina.

France was considered an imperialist nation, as were such countries as Belgium, Germany, and England. Such nations want the natural resources of other countries and they often take the resources by force and exploit the local populations. They also attempt to spread their cultures, thinking their ways are superior to all others. Their beliefs in Christianity are especially brutal and they attempt to stamp out all other religions refusing to accept such long held beliefs as Buddhism, Hinduism, and others.

Such nations also invade weak countries for fear that if they do not, others will and they will lose any opportunities to gain the natural resources for their own use. France especially wanted Vietnam's rich coal mines. They wanted to supply coal to ships in Asian waters and to export it to other countries.

The French soon divided Vietnam into three separate colonies: Tonkin, in the north; Annam, in the center; and Cochin China, in the south. They allowed the Vietnamese emperor to remain in power as a figurehead to help pacify the people. France sent several officials to Vietnam to run the new territory. They knew nothing of the people, the language, the culture, or the country. Since they felt superior they felt no need to learn anything about them; the Vietnamese had only to listen and to obey. The French used Vietnamese, called "culture brokers", to help run the country.

Vietnamese traditionally worked their own land. The French consolidated them into large tracts of land while the power brokers often confiscated tracts for themselves. Over half the farmland in Vietnam was eventually controlled by about 900 landowners.

Rice production increased, but the French exported it to other parts of the world while the Vietnamese often went hungry. The French introduced rubber trees into the country and Vietnamese were often forced to work the plantations. Many died due to poor working conditions and poor food. The coal industry was improved, again at a cost. Miners worked for the equivalent of 20 to 30 cents a day.

In 1897, Paul Doumer was appointed governor-general of Indochina. He gained complete control of salt, alcohol, and opium. He built a new opium refinery and made efforts to addict the people to increase revenues. Eventually one-third of French colonial income came from opium.

The Vietnamese had not given up on their fight for independence and former Emperor Ham Nghi led a revolt named the "Scholar's Revolt" because the uprising was supported by many university educated patriots. The revolt lasted about ten years, but eventually Ham Nghi was captured and exiled. The French acted brutally to subdue the revolt destroying entire villages, throwing thousands of people into prisons, and executing many people by guillotine. Severed heads were placed in baskets and placed onto the streets to be claimed by family members.

Within several years another revolt, led by mandarins Phan Boi Chau and his friend, Phan Chu Trinh, broke out. They decided to poison French military officers. When the uprising failed they planned a general insurrection. Peasant farmers had started to protest and he thought he could inspire them to fight. Because the men were mandarins, their support came mostly from the educated classes and several businessmen. The revolt failed and Phan Boi Chau was imprisoned. Trinh was sentenced for execution, but was eventually exiled to France.

Phan Chu Trinh had petitioned the government in France for reform. He wanted democracy for the country, fewer taxes, and industrialization. He was especially adamant about increased education. Few Vietnamese could read or write and there was only one University at Hanoi. Trinh continued his work in France and gathered a small following of supporters including Nguyen Sinh Cung, a young man who would eventually be named Ho Chi Minh.

Ho Chi Minh was born in 1890 in the village of Hoang Tru where his father, Nguyen Sinh Sach, taught school. Sach also wanted freedom for Vietnam and it was here that Ho Chi Minh met patriot Phan Boi Chau. Ho Chi Minh was attending the National Academy in Hue when Chau started his rebellion. Because Chau visited the family many times, Ho was expelled from school.

Ho Chi Minh found work as a teacher in the south, but the French kept him under constant surveillance. Using an assumed name, he managed to slip away by working on a ship where he sailed about the world stopping to work in many countries including India, Africa, the United States, France, and England. While visiting many of these countries he observed the miserable conditions of the poor often brought about because of the greed inherent in capitalism. He wanted something better for his country.

He developed a great respect for America and her people. He felt that they truly believed in freedom and that if anyone might help the Vietnamese people, it would be them. Several times in his life he wrote the U.S. government for assistance to gain freedom.

Ho eventually moved to France where a large Vietnamese community existed. He sought help and advice from the patriot Phan Chu Trinh. Trinh gave him a job in his photography shop. In 1919 Ho started the Association of Annamite Patriots in an effort to oppose French rule in Vietnam. He quickly became a leader among his people. He spent much time with Vietnamese workers and encouraged them to demand higher wages in French factories.

A peace conference was held at Versailles at the end of World War One. U.S. President Wilson called for changes to make the world more equitable which, in turn, might lessen the chances of future wars. Ho attended the conference and presented his manifesto for Vietnam.

Asking for freedom of religion and freedom of the press, he also listed his grievances against the French and wanted them to end their monopolies on various goods including salt, and opium. At this point he changed his name to Nguyen Ai Quoc, meaning Nguyen the Patriot. Because this manifesto alerted the police to his revolutionary beliefs, he was again put under surveillance.

Russia, engaged in their own fight for freedom, was one of the few countries to support Ho's beliefs in Vietnamese independence. Many people believed communism was a better alternative to other forms of government. Ho started to seriously study the movement. He eventually believed that communism would help free his people so he joined the French Communist Party and quickly, with his congenial and intelligent personality, rose to become one of the leaders. The new Soviet Union soon recognized him as a leader and thought he might help spread their doctrine throughout Southeast Asia. He was flown to Moscow where he studied at the Communist University of the Toilers of the East.

Ho constantly reminded various communist leaders of the opportunity to spread their political system in Asia. He said the peasants were ready for revolt; they just needed some help since fighting the French would be very difficult.

Ho Chi Minh

Ho Chi Minh was first sent to China to work with revolutionaries. From his base in Canton, China, he started a revolutionary organization in Vietnam named the Vietnamese Revolutionary Youth League. He brought the new recruits to China for training then returned them to Vietnam to spread the doctrine of revolution.

Little had changed in Vietnam during this time, adding to the anger of the people. Most decent jobs went to French immigrants; more than 500,000 peasant farmers owned no land because the French had secured most of the fertile land; and fewer than 5,000 children graduated from school. To help with his revolutionary ideas, Ho wrote many articles concerning freedom and independent rule and started the Vietnamese Communist Party in 1930 to further his beliefs. Due to the worldwide depression, more Vietnamese suffered and turned to Ho for hope.

During World War Two, Japan invaded Vietnam. Because France had already lost the war to Germany, an ally of Japan, France was still allowed to govern Vietnam. Many French soldiers, especially the French Foreign Legion, did not agree and fought against the Japanese as they retreated to safety in China.

If the Vietnamese thought they might be treated better under the Japanese, they were mistaken. The Japanese proved even more brutal than the French. So much food was stolen to feed Japanese forces that the Vietnamese soon started to starve. In the confusion of war, Ho saw an opportunity to launch his revolution. Again he sought the help of the United States.

American President Roosevelt insisted that all the allied countries agree to free their colonies after the war. He claimed it was hypocritical to fight for democracy and freedom against the Germans and Japanese while the allies kept people under oppression. They reluctantly agreed with the exception of France who claimed that French Indochina was not capable of governing themselves. Roosevelt insisted they relinquish their Asian holdings but agreed to give them time to work out a favorable solution to everyone involved.

The U.S. decided to help Ho Chi Minh in his fight for freedom if Ho used his forces against the Japanese. (He was now using the name Ho Chi Minh meaning "He Who Enlightens.") Major Thompson and a group of American specialists were sent to train the new Vietnamese forces under General Giap. When they arrived at a cave near the village of Tan Trao, they found Ho gravely ill. They did not expect him to live. The American medic with the unit, Paul Hoagland, nursed him back to health.

Major Thompson and his newly trained Vietnamese force attacked and defeated the Japanese at Thai Nguyen. Because the war had just ended, Ho and General Giap decided the time was ripe to start their revolution. Their new group was called the Viet Minh.

British soldiers moved into the south of Vietnam while Chinese soldiers moved into the north. Ho Chi Minh and his Viet Minh marched into Hanoi and declared independence. France insisted the country be returned to them. Prime Minister Churchill believed in colonialism and agreed to help France regain control of the country. In order to keep the Viet Minh from occupying the south, he allowed British troops to rearm the Japanese to help keep out the Vietnamese until the French could return and establish themselves.

In the north the Chinese were running rampant. They considered their occupation the perfect opportunity to loot everything of value from the country. The Vietnamese forces were too weak to deal with them.

President Truman was now head of the U.S. government after the death of President Roosevelt. He had little interest in Vietnam although he suggested Vietnam eventually be given their independence.

Ho Chi Minh still believed in the American people and their concept of freedom. On September 2, 1945, he spoke to the Vietnamese people. In the speech he said, "We hold the truth that all men are created equal, that they are endowed by their creator with certain unalienable rights, among them life, liberty, and the pursuit of happiness." He often used parts of American speeches, but if he thought the United States would come to his defense, he was mistaken. Instead he eventually asked the French for help.

With the French, he worked out a peace agreement. Help him get the Chinese out of Vietnam and he would agree to split Vietnam in half. The French could control the south and Ho would control the north. Until the eventual reunification, after two wars for independence, the countries would be known as North Vietnam and South Vietnam.

The peace did not last long. The French needed time to build up their forces in the south and were looking for an excuse to invade the north. They found that excuse over a minor import disagreement in Haiphong. France launched an attack against Hanoi and drove out Ho and the Viet Minh. From 2,000 to 4,000 civilians were killed in the attack. A brutal war lasting 8 years followed with Russia and China supporting the Viet Minh and the United States reluctantly supporting the French.

Although America still believed in freedom for Ho Chi Minh and the Vietnamese, they were against communism. The French also blackmailed the U.S. to gain support. Western Europe needed a strong line of defense against the communists of Eastern Europe. France said they would not join the Western alliance unless the U.S. supported them in Vietnam. The United States started sending them guns, planes, ammunition, food, and eventually paid for 80% to 90% of the war. The C.I.A. supplied an air force consisting of transport planes, mechanics and pilots. The air force was named Civil Air Transport, or CAT. During the siege of Dien Bien Phu American CAT pilots were paid a minimum of $4,200 a month, a healthy amount in the 1950's and one of America's most colorful pilots, "Earth- quake" McGoon, was shot down and killed during the battle.

With the outbreak of the Korean War, the French pressed the United States for continued aid claiming they were the last defense against the communists in Asia.

Victories on both sides of the conflict were inconsistent. One thing was certain: both sides fought a bitter and cruel war with no quarter given. Both sides were ruthless; both sides committed atrocities; and both sides appeared fearless.

The French, although better equipped, suffered from little popular sup- port. French citizens had grown tired of the war and they started protest- ing in the streets of Paris for an end to the war. The government claimed they wanted to win the war, but often refused to support the troops and held back equipment and reinforcements. While the United States gave support, the French government often sold French equipment, including airplanes, to other countries. Native French soldiers were not required to fight outside of France so colonial soldiers, from places like Algeria and Morocco and anxious for their own freedom, were fighting the war. About half of all French forces were native Vietnamese and Montagnards from various hill tribes. The Foreign Legion supplied the strongest units. Moral was often very low with the colinial forces.

The Viet Minh had the opposite problem. Because they were fighting for independence, their moral was often very high and they had popular support. What they lacked was arms, especially heavy guns. They had no air force, no navy, no armor, and few transportation vehicles. Many small villages set up forges to hand-build weapons.

Then there was the problem of leadership. The French lacked a cohesive plan and consistent management. The French government constantly equivocated on their views of the situation and Generals, with different ideas about winning the conflict, constantly changed. Eight years of war brought four different Generals: Leclerc, de Tassigny, Salan, and Navarre.

General Vo Nguyen Giap

Viet Minh leadership remained consistent. Ho Chi Minh had a single focus, freeing his country, and a General, Vo Nguyen Giap, to bring that focus about, not just with the French, but also later with the Americans.

Unlike the French Generals trained in the finest military colleges, Giap, with a graduate degree in law, was a history professor, and self-taught military leader. He constantly studied the tactics of Napoleon and the theories on war by Clausewitz. He had every reason to hate the French. He had been imprisoned for his revolutionary beliefs. His wife, sister, father, and sister-in-law were also arrested, tortured, and killed by the French. His daughter died in prison from neglect. During the war he learned from his mistakes and, unlike the French, seldom made them twice.

From the beginning, the French had difficulty engaging the Viet Minh in a set-piece battle. The Viet Minh preferred to fight using hit-and-run tactics. Fighting a European type battle would result in disaster. The French, with all of their equipment, would simply overwhelm them. The Viet Minh attacked quickly then melted into the countryside before the French could launch any counter-attacks.

The French managed to catch many Viet Minh at Bac Kan, killing about 9,000 and briefly demoralizing them. Giap continued his guerilla tactics as he rebuilt his forces. He caused so many small defeats near the Chinese border that the French decided they could no longer hold the area. They decided to abandon their strongpoints along Colonial Highway Number 4 and move them closer to Hanoi. Their idea was to retreat from their farthest fort at Cao Bang and gather up the other forts along the way.

Giap learned of the plan and launched a major offensive striking the outpost at Dong Khe. Nearly 7,000 French troops were engaged in the fighting. Only about 100 survived giving the Viet Minh a tremendous victory. Giap became over-confident and launched a major attack against a garrison of 6,000 French Foreign Legionnaires at Vinh Yen. Forced to fight in the open the battle proved to be a total disaster for the Viet Minh. Giap lost almost 14,000 men killed, wounded, and captured.

Not to be discouraged, Giap launched another attack against Mao Khe followed by an attack on Phat Diem. Both times the Viet Minh were defeated. (The battle at Phat Diem was later mentioned in the movie "The Quiet American.")

General de Lattre, the best of the French Generals to serve in Vietnam, encouraged by French victories launched his own attacks driving the Viet Minh from the Red River Delta then capturing the city of Hoa Binh 25 miles from Hanoi.

The fire of freedom burned strongly with the Viet Minh and they soon recaptured Hoa Binh. General Salan replaced General de Lattre, suffering from cancer and depression at the death of his son in a jungle battle near Ninh Binh. Salan was a competent General, but not brilliant and his forces started to suffer. Small outposts started to fall.

Giap overran outposts along Nghia Lo and captured most of the land along the Black River Valley. Only the airfield at Na San managed to hold out. Na San was an experiment by the French to see if they could hold a fort in a remote area and supply it by air. They were successful and managed to hold off Giap's repeated attacks. The French victory would prove disastrous later when General Navarre decided to build another such fort at Dien Bien Phu. It was also instrumental in Giap's decision to do battle at Dien Bien Phu. He believed the reason he had not defeated the fort at Na San was because he had launched his attack too soon. He had not gathered enough forces, and equipment. He would not make that mistake again.

In 1953, Salan was replaced with General Navarre, a man who had never visited Vietnam, knew nothing of the will of the Vietnamese or their fighting tactics, had no idea about the countryside, the language, or the culture. None of this concerned him. He was a professional soldier. Nothing else mattered.

He was sent to Vietnam and told to keep status quo - no battles, nothing risky, defend yourself if necessary, but do not launch any operations. France was tired of the war and finally realized that a diplomatic solution must be reached even if it meant freeing Vietnam. A conference was being scheduled for the following year in Geneva. Navarre disregarded the instructions. He wanted to defeat the Viet Minh in a large battle to give the

French a better bargaining position at the conference. If he could lure the Viet Minh into a fight, he could defeat them. He wanted to offer them a "French Carrot," a small force Giap might find too inviting to resist. When the Viet Minh attacked, he would crush them with superior firepower. What he needed was an air base, so his army could be supplied, in a valley distant from Hanoi. He chose the valley of Dien Bien Phu.

Navarre felt several problems might be solved with the occupation of the valley.

1. He could prevent the Viet Minh from entering Laos
2. He could capture large rice and opium fields thus depriving the Viet Minh of both food and money they were earning from the sale of opium to buy arms
3. He could launch attacks into the hills and disrupt supplies
4. He might draw General Giap into a large conventional battle

Like most Generals, he craved winning a major battle, so drawing the Viet Minh into a fight was what drew his concentration.

When given details of the operation, to be named "Castor," most of his subordinates thought the gamble too risky. Even General Cogny, his commander in Northern Vietnam, reluctantly agreed to the plan as long as the main purpose of the operation was offensive. As the General who would directly command the opoeration, he viewed Dien Bien Phu as a staging area for thrusts into the hills. Navarre agreed, although he had no intent of honoring that agreement. As the battle unfolded these two Generals eventually refused to communicate.

One of the staunchest opponents to the operation was Colonel Nicot, commander of the French air force. Dien Bien Phu was too far from supplies in Hanoi and his transport planes had just enough fuel to fly there and return. He also had too few transport planes and too few flight crews. Every available plane would be needed to keep the base supplied, an impossible task considering the planes were also needed in other parts of Northern Vietnam. The planes also needed constant repair and any anti-aircraft guns dragged to the area might cause great damage. Navarre disregarded any opposition, including the advice of seasoned Vietnam officers who understood the Viet Minh and the country, and on November 20, 1953, he launched his plan.

French landing

A more disgruntled group of French officers involved in the operation would be difficult to imagine. As stated, General Cogny thought the air base a poor plan unless it was used as a staging point, not a defensive one.

General Guilles was charged with the initial attack. He had been commander of the Na San base. Although his defense was successful, he understood it was only because of luck. That base had two complete lines of defense and even then, the outer line was breached. He knew that if General Giap had more resources, he would have overrun the French. Guilles refused to take charge of Dien Bien Phu unless Navarre agreed to relieve him as soon as possible. Guilles said, "I refuse to die in this hell hole."

The man who relieved him was Colonel Christian de Castries, a brave, heroic, and career soldier from an aristocratic background. He was a tank commander, a champion equestrian rider, and a fighter pilot. He was wounded in World War Two and twice in Vietnam. He was a man of tremendous courage - and the wrong man for the job. He protested the assignment. As a tank commander he understood his limitations with a static position. He needed room to maneuver. He felt unqualified for the task. He was right. Navarre refused to listen. During the entire siege, de Castries refused to leave his bunker. He ate all his specially prepared meals at a table set with fine silver cutlery, a linen tablecloth, and lit with candlelight. In the evenings he played cards with his other officers. He even installed a bathtub. The bathtub is on display in the museum. He completely froze during the battle and was incapable of making a decision.

If General Navarre thought he could lure General Giap into a large battle he was right. Giap was well aware of Navarre's plan and decided to use it to his advantage. His greatest asset was French arrogance. They felt themselves superior to the Vietnamese and were unconcerned when making decisions. They built their air base in a valley protected by strongpoints on several low hills totally disregarding the one thing that every common infantryman knows: take the high ground. They left the high hills and mountains to the Viet Minh knowing they could not install any artillery in such rough terrain. If they managed to get a few guns there, they could not be supplied; and if they did fire a few rounds, the French guns of Colonel Piroth would blow them apart because French gunners were far superior.

Any force Giap managed to bring to the area could also not be supplied. His supplies would have to come from China, almost 500 miles away. The French had their airstrip and could easily be supplied. In fact, they counted entirely on the airstrip for all their needs and never imagined the Viet Minh destroying the runway.

The French were also bringing their best units to the fight: Legionnaires and Paratroopers, some of the finest soldiers in the world. To think they might be beaten by a mass of ill trained farmers was laughable. Forget the fact that the Viet Minh had occasionally been beating them throughout

Vietnam; those were minor flukes. Eventually about 14,000 French served in the valley, only about 6,000 combat troops, the rest support troops.

General Giap knew all of this and set about destroying each myth. He made sure his soldiers did not get cocky but remained levelheaded. The victories they had won were great for moral, but arrogance got you killed. Be competent, not superior.

Take the high ground and fill it with artillery. Vietnamese never think they cannot do something. If they are told to drag artillery up mountains by hand, they just do it without question. Giap felt the French were in a bowl. He need only stand on the rim to destroy them. He managed to install almost 200 heavy weapons above 57mm. The French had just over fifty.

He also felt it was the French who could not be supplied. Knock out their airstrip and they were finished. Again, he never thought he could not be supplied regardless of how distant his supply line. Fifty miles, 100 miles, 500 miles, it made no difference to him. He immediately set 100,00 to 300,000 coolies to work hacking roads through the jungle and carrying supplies. The Russians also gave him 100 to 400 trucks. (Firm statistics are always difficult to obtain from the Viet Minh side. Numbers are often given based on several established histories.)

The French badly overestimated the quality of their troops. Over half their numbers were Vietnamese and local T'ai. Although they often fought extremely well, they occasionally had trouble. Even their elite forces, including the Foreign Legion, were half native troops. The elite forces were also not quite as elite as the French thought, mostly because they were tired and worn down through constant action. They had been continously tossed into one fight after another. What they needed was a rest, not another difficult battle.

General Giap also brought his best units to the battle including the feared 312th Infantry Division under General Le Trong Tan and the 308th Infantry Division under General Vuong Thua Vu. In all Giap threw 50,000 combat troops into the fight.

The Viet Minh had been using Dien Bien Phu as a rest and training area and several units were there when the French landed. About 100 were killed and wounded as the French occupied the valley while the French lost nine killed. The French were immediately conflicted. Were they to fortify the valley in a defensive position, as General Navarre wanted, or launch aggressive attacks into the hills as general Cogny wanted? They had too few troops to do both effectively. As a result they attempted both and failed at each.

The forays into the hills met with little effect and accomplished nothing except to show that the Viet Minh were quickly surrounding the Valley. They were eventually ringed so tightly they could not venture any farther

then their artillery could carry.

Building fortifications was a disaster. The combat troops were too exhausted to dig holes after fighting in the hills. And there was not enough material to build adequate

Patrols into the hills

fortifications and shelters. The elite troops almost refused to build shelters claiming they were offensive soldiers and would not sit in the mud like pigs.

Exploring the Battlefield
the siege

The Valley as pilots saw it when approaching from the north.

The Viet Minh launched their attack at 1700 hours (5:00PM) on March 13, 1954. The shelling was deafening and came as a surprise, not the attack itself for French Intelligence had predicted it almost to the minute, but the ferocity. The entire Valley erupted as the earth rose up in protest. The French never imagined that Giap had so many heavy guns.

Colonel Piroth immediately started his counter-batter fire, but he could not find the Viet Mnh guns. Standard artillery practice is to place guns behind hills and mountains, to protect them, and fire over the crests using artillery spotters to direct fire. Piroth started firing over the hills and mountains to knock out the guns. Fighter-bombers were also called in to scour the hills.

Giap had foreseen this and had placed his guns into fortifications dug into the facing hillsides. He needed no spotters. Each gun battery saw the entire Valley and directed fire as needed. Even if Colonel Piroth had found the guns, they were completely protected. Not s single Viet Minh gun was destroyed during the battle. French guns were totally exposed and quickly started to disintegrate.

Colonel Piroth had decided to place his guns on the Valley floor, and without protection. Because he needed to cover the entire Valley, he wanted them to swing in all 360 degrees. In order to do this, any protection, except for a low row of ineffective sandbags, was discarded. Not just his guns, but also more importantly, his gunners, were exposed.

French 155 gun in its curcular enclosure. Several guns are on display near their original firing positions behind Colonel de Castries bunker in the Center of Resistance. All guns were exposed to Viet Minh fire and artillery crews suffered terrible casualties.

The defense of the Valley lay largely with Colonel Piroth and his input helped establish the various positions. Many artillery officers warned him that his guns were too few, but he ignored them. Because his guns could swing in all direction he felt he needed fewer of them. One French government official, visiting the fort, reminded him that there were hundreds of unused guns in Hanoi and he could have as many as he liked. He declined claiming they would just get in the way. Three days after the start of the siege he became despondant and wandered from unit to unit apologizing for his mistakes.

The Center of Resistance, just West of the Nam Yum River, held the main command post, most of the artillery, the key hospital, the cemetery, various electrical generators, water purification units, and the shock troops of the 1st Foreign Legion Paratroop and the 8th

Unprotected French guns during the battle

Parachute Assault used for counter-attacks. Several fighter-bombers and spotter planes stood surrounded by sandbags near the southern end of the airstrip.

De Castries bunker in its original position near the main artillery batteries

The eastern and western defenses, separated by the Nam Yum River, were connected with a Bailey bridge capable of supporting supply, trucks, and tanks. The original bridge is still in operation.

Bailey bridge still in use

The Viet Minh soon concentrated their fire on strong-post Beatrice (Him Lam) north east of the Center. Beatrice consists of 3 hills and was occupied by the 3/13 Foreign Legion Half-

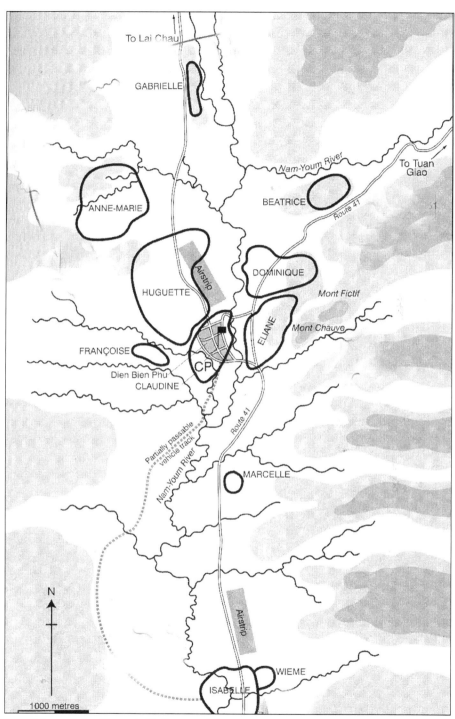

Map of the French Valley positions at the start of the siege

Brigade, one of the strongest units in the Valley. Giap knew if he could overrun the position, the remaining French units would be demoralized so the position was more important from a psychological position rather than a strategic one. The Viet Minh often chose psychological objectives to attain goals, something the French seldom did.

The 3/13 Foreign Legion Half-Brigade had never lost a battle during their history and they were the envy of many units. During World War Two they had been consistently given almost impossible missions, and they always came through. Fighting in North Africa they had stopped Rommel's Afrika Korps at Bir-Hakeim long enough for Britain's 8th Army to escape and establish a new defensive position.

Major Pegot, a battle-hardened professional, commanded the position and was respected by his men. Because building materials were scarce, the entire hillside had been stripped bare of vegetation so the Viet Minh saw every position. The entire Valley needed 36,000 tons of building materials for adequate protection. By stripping the villages and close hillsides, they managed to collect about 2,000 leaving them short by about 34,000 tons. That shortage became quickly apparent as the bunkers started to collapse under Viet Minh fire.

Beatrice before the opening shots

The Valley was divided into different commands. Beatrice fell under the command of Colonel Goucher's Mobile Group 9. Major Pegot reported directly to him. The 3/13 had been reduced from 700 men to about

One hill of Beatrice today

500, the others being used to keep Road 41 open to the Center of Resistance open. One lieutenant per company, plus sergeants, commanded the position. Centered in the middle of the three hills was the command post of Major Pegot and his staff.

Beatrice was so tightly surrounded on the morning of the battle, Major Jean Chenel's 2nd T'ai had to fight hand-to-hand to keep Road 41 open to the strongpoint. As soon as they withdrew, the Viets immediately moved in. The Center of Resistance had its own problems. For the last two days they needed a full battalion, sup-

The fortifications of Beatrice are being slowly restored

ported by two tank platoons, just to get drinking water. Hours before the opening shots, Major Pegot radioed Colonel Goucher that his men were tired and nervous and in no shape to fight.

Colonel Langlais was the commander above Colonel Goucher so the command in this section was from de Castries to Langlais to Goucher to

The trail to Beatrice is access-
able from Him Lam and is not
marked

Pegot. As the attack started Colonel Langlais radioed Majors Guiraud and Tourret, commanders of the First Foreign Legion Parachute Battalion and the 8th Assault used for counter-attacks, but the lines were cut. He established radio contact just as his command post suffered a direct hit. The 8 men present were all buried under dirt and timbers but were largely unhurt. Within minutes another shell landed – a dud that smoked at their feet.

The Viet Minh 141 and 219 Regiments of the 312th Division pressed hard their attack and refused to back down. Squad Leader Phan Dinh Giot

23

threw himself against the opening of a machinegun bunker sacrificing himself to save his attacking forces.

Thirty minutes after the start of the battle Colonel Goucher learned

An abondoned house sits near the command bunker of Major Pegot

that Major Pegot, and his entire staff had been killed. Beatrice was now leaderless. Goucher established radio contact with the different companies and learned that the Legionnaires were continuing to fight. He called a meeting in his bunker to pick a new commander calling his chief of staff, Major Vadot and his staff in from a separate bunker. He had kept the commands in two separate bunkers so they would not be wiped out in case of a direct hit, but time was of the essence so they were called together. The bunker was so crowded that Major Vadot climbed onto the mattress of Goucher's bunk. The mattress saved his life. A Viet Minh shell bounced down the airshaft and exploded at Colonel Goucher's feet killing everyone except Vadot. Goucher lay on the floor, both arms blown off and his legs and chest crushed. When Father Trinquand arrived, he asked him for a drink of water. Two Foreign Legionnaires took him to the surgery but he died as Chief Chaplain Father Heinrich administered last rites.

With all French commanders dead, Beatrice was finished. Sergeant Kubiak took command of 9th Company and managed to hold out for another two hours. Kubiak was the luckiest man in Dien Bien Phu. He survived every major fight, often saving his fellow soldiers. The strongpoint radioed the artillery to drop all available rounds on the position. Kubiak took what survivors he could find and hid out in the nearby brush into morning.

The last message from the strongpoint came from 11th Company at 2100 hours. "Viets all over the place." The radio went silent.

Machinegun bunker on Beatrice

Colonel de Castries faults now started to appear. He swarmed with indecision. He did not know if he should launch a counter-attack. Colonel Langlais said one should be launched immediately. De Castries hesitated and did not decide until the morning. Even then he was not sure. He moved his troops slowly toward the position. Perhaps the strongpoint was too costly to recapture and to hold. Was it even necessary to the defense of the airstrip? And what of the airstrip? The Viet Minh guns had rendered it useless. The French means of supply, the one thing on which they counted, was gone. Within several days it was shut down completely.

As soon as the French advanced they came under heavy fire. Suddenly it stopped. Lieutenant Turpin, of 11th Company, badly wounded and carrying a white flag, met them with a message from Commander Le Trong Tan from the 312th Division. The Commander offered a truce to allow the French to pick up any wounded survivors from Beatrice. The message was relayed to de Casries. He could not decide. He radioed General Congy in Hanoi for advice. Cogny agreed.

The truce may not have been to the advantage of the French. Giap was again employing psychological warfare. The French could not decline the offer without demoralizing their troops. The tactic also stopped the counter-attack. The delay gave Giap's troops time to redeploy. Only a few survivors were found on the hills and the French retreated back to the Center of Resistance leaving Beatrice to the Viet Minh. De Castries knew Giap would attack Gabrielle (Doc Lap) next.

Viet Minh hauling guns up hills

Giap had done his work well. Thousands of villagers had hauled tons of food and ammunition to the battle site. Some Russian trucks were used but French bicycles carried most of the supplies. Workers strapped long bamboo poles to one of the handlebars so a villager could walk beside the bike and keep it balanced. A bike could hold about 400 pounds. All the supplies were deposited at Tuan Giao, fifty miles from the Valley. Everything was carried by hand over those last 50 miles.

Artillery pieces were hauled inch by inch up steep hillsides and newly hacked trails and dug deeply into caves for protection where they were pulled out to fire then pushed back inside when finished. The big guns were placed on the eastern hills and the heavy mortars, easier to transport, on the farther western hills.

The 5/7 Algerian Rifles on Gabrielle were tense, yet confident. They felt they were better troops than the Legionnaires and they had a long-standing rivalry. They also had the strongest position in the Valley, the only one with two lines of defense, and had won a contest sponsored by de Castries to prove it. The

Most Viet supplies were carried by bicycle

hill was first named the Torpedo because of the shape, and only later named Gabrielle to conform with the other names. They had recently suffered a number of difficulties.

Like Beatrice, Gabrielle was slowly being cut off from the Center of Resistance. On March 12th, a day before the siege began, Lieutenant Botella, trying to keep the road open, lost ten men at the river crossing of Khe Phai. This main road was the only way to send in reinforcements if needed.

Lieutenant Moreau sent his company north only to discover a web of approach trenches dug to within 200 meters of his position. He was fortunate to discover a Viet Minh map showing all the trenches, which he sent to de Castries so the artillery might zero in on them.

A clean row of steps leads to Gabrielle north just off the Pavie track

They were now being shelled rather constantly and no one was sure if they might be attacked first rather than Beatrice. At 1600 hours (4:PM) on the day of the siege, Lieutenant Chauveau, the battalion doctor, was wounded. Doctor Dechelotte, dodging shells the entire way, fought his way in a jeep from the Center to the position to take charge. He did not last long and was wounded around 1900 hours (7:PM). Fortunately, the following day, another doctor was found, Sergeant Soldati, who had enlisted as a French Foreign Legionnaire. He was the last man to arrive before the attack.

As the siege began another development occurred. The Hills around Gabrielle came alive with Viet Minh anti-aircraft fire. No one expected them to have these guns and they immediately started firing on the aircraft on the field and on approaches and landings.

Dr. Grauwin, chief doctor of the entire camp, ordered another surgical team dropped into the valley. Because of the new anti-aircraft fire the pilot became confused and dropped the team directly into the barbed wire where, under fire, they cut their way out.

Major Kah had just assumed command of Gabrielle from Major de Mecquenem, but de Mecquenem decided to stay on until Kah was completely familiar with the strongpoint. Knowing they would be hit next, they issued food and ammunition to last 4 days of continuous combat and returned the Vietnamese prisoners, who were working to build positions, to the Valley. A hot meal was served that afternoon. They were assured that a C-47 would drop flares to light the battlefield through the night. Colonel Piroth promised continuous artillery support even though a quarter of all

About half of French forces were Vietnamese

rounds had already been fired in support of Beatrice. The command post was divided into two areas, just as Colonel Goucher had done.

At 1800 hours (6:PM) Viet Minh mortars opened up from Ban Na Ten just two kilometers distant. Within hours the heavy weapons bunkers of Lieutenant Moreau's 4th Company were destroyed. Moreau, killed in his command post, had been anxious to see his wife who had arrived in Hanoi several days earlier.

Lieutenant Clerge, commander of the heavy mortars of the 5th Foreign

Russian filmmakers restaged the battle of Beatrice for propoganda reasons

Legion Regiment, had his radio destroyed. He worked his way to the officer's mess, where the second Gabrielle command post had been placed, to use theirs.

The Viet Minh attacked with regiments of the 88th and 102nd from the 308th People's Army Division giving them at least an eight to one advantage over the French. 4th Company was about to be overrun when a counter attack was launched led by Sergeants Lobut and Rouzic. Rouzic, the driver for French gangster Perrot-le-Fou, had joined the Legion to escape the police. They managed to stabilize the line but, after several hours of fighting, and being outflanked, finally withdrew. Only seven of his men remained.

Piroth, true to his word, kept up a murderous fire on the Viets and suddenly, at 0230 hours (2:30AM) the Viet Minh attack halted. Major de Mecquenem reported to de Castries then passed the command to Major Kah.

An hour later the attack resumed as new Viet Minh batteries opened up from the northeast almost doubling the fire. Gunner Pham Van

The number of Viet Minh antiaircraft guns came as a surprise to the French

Tuy had hand-built his own 75mm weapon and dragged it into position where he destroyed a French machine gun bunker.

1st Company's commander, Captain Narby, was soon killed and his lieutenant badly wounded. The remaining mortars on Gabrielle were quickly destroyed. The same mistake made by Colonel Goucher was now made on Gabrielle as the remaining commanders gathered in the same bunker, just as a shell entered, blowing off one of Major Kah's legs and riddling de Mecquenem with shrapnel. (Some officers were not aware the other officers were there.) The shell also destroyed the command radios. Gabrielle was now without an upper command.

Command of the remaining forces fell to de Mecquenem's deputy, but he laid shivering and crying in a corner, his nerves totally shot. Captain Gendre took command, found a working radio in the command post of 3rd Company, and radioed de Castries for an immediate counter-attack. De Castries ordered him to hold out at all costs as he gathered forces for a counter-attack.

De Castries' equivocation again came into play. He ordered Major Seguin-Pazzis to launch a counter-attack using a company from the First Foreign Legion Parachute Battalion, the newly arrived 5th Vietnamese Airborne Battalion, and the tank squadron of Captain Hervouet. The Vietnamese paratroopers were in no shape to fight. They had just landed and had been trying to get some rest in the mud when they were ordered into the attack. They froze after coming under fire at Ban Ke Phai.

De Castries issued three different sets of orders: attack, retreat, and move ahead without attacking and retrieve the retreating units from Gabrielle. Gabrielle was only able to pick up bits and pieces of radio conversations. What they heard was to retreat to the advancing French forces. Although Captain Gendre felt the position could be held, he abandoned the strongpoint and came off the hillside. Two positions had now been lost in as many days. Ann-Marie was next.

Memorial on Gabrielle

The low hills of Ann-Marie as seen from Garielle. The position consisted of several small hills named numerically.

Ann-Marie, to the west, proved an easy victory for the Viet Minh and was taken almost without a shot being fired. The 3rd T'ai Infantry battalion, supported by the 1st Foreign Legion Composite Mortar Company, held the position. The T'ai soldiers had been recruited from mountain villages. Their understanding was that they would defend their local territory. They had now been sent to this Valley where they had no interest in fighting while the Viet Minh were taking over their villages. They decided to leave and started slipping away into the jungle.

T'ai soldiers fought well at Na San but fell apart at Dien Bien Phu

Meanwhile, the supply situation had become desperate. Already the French had fired 12,600 rounds of 105; 10,000 rounds of 120-mm mortar; and 3,000 rounds of 155. Since the airstrip was unusable, the supplies needed to be dropped by parachute. New drop zones were established. Ammunition, food, and medical supplies started falling from the sky. Replacements fell for 1 BEP and the 8th Assault, three complete gun crews, another doctor - Lieutenant Rivier – and Major Bigeard with his 6th Parachute Battalion.

Bigeard was a fighting legend in Vietnam. Totally fearless, he went into battle unarmed and carrying nothing more than a short stick. He was a great tactician and just his presence raised the moral of the beleaguered troops. In many ways, the French held out so long because of him.

De Castries staff was starting to fall apart. His Chief of Staff, Lieutenant Colonel Keller, suffered a nervous breakdown, and his paratroop officers were ready to revolt because of de Castries indecision. Eventually they took command from him, al-

Fighting legend Major Biegard

though headquarters in Hanoi was not informed of the revolt. Command fell to Colonel Langlais who led the battle until the end. He and his officers became known as the "Paratroop Mafia." He was also fearless, respected by his men, and he constantly traveled from strongpoint to strongpoint to encourage them while Colonel de Castries remained hidden underground.

The artillery commander, Colonel Piroth, also fell apart. As previously mentioned, he wandered from unit to unit apologizing for his inability to stop the Viet Minh guns. On the third day of the siege he staggared back to his command post on the east side of the river near the Bailey bridge and placed a hand grenade to his chest. Because of falling moral, his suicide was not reported to Hanoi for several days.

The Viet Minh continued to play their psychological games and offered

Colonel Piroth memorial sits in the middle of the market at is original comand post

to return 86 wounded survivors from Gabrielle. De Castries had no choice but to take them. Giap knew that the French wounded could no longer be evacuated and that treating them would become a great burden and quicken their defeat. He, in return, refused to take back any wounded Viet Minh so the

French not only treated their own, but also his.

By March 17th practically all of Ann-Marie was deserted except for a few loyal T'ai and a handful of Legionnaires under the command of Captain Desire. Desire was willing to hand on, but feeling the position could no longer be defended, Ann-Marie was abandoned, except for two smaller hills that were renamed Huguette 6 and 7. Their fates awaited a future date although the results would be the same.

The air force fuel supplies exploded but another surgical team managed to arrive safely. General Cogny, circling in an airplane over the Valley, refused to attempt a landing and take charge of the battle, so one of the greatest sieges in history was left in the hands of two Colonels.

Colonel Langlais and his Paratroop Mifia

Another concern was the safety of all the women in the camp. Native soldiers had brought many of their families with them. Also in the camp were the women of two Mobile Bordellos, who eventually volunteered as nurses to care for the wounded, and a T'ai ballet company.

The siege now settled into a constant slugfest with one Viet Minh attack followed by another and each attack countered by the French. By the middle of April the French had been reduced to about 3,500 combat troops and were on half rations, then third rations. Ammunition was scarce. Giap had his forces dig approach trenches ever closer to French positions and one by one they started to fall reducing the defensive perimeter. Because of the murderous anti-aircraft fire French pilots flew ever higher. Over 50 airplanes were hit, many of them crashing. Parachute drops became totally inaccurate to the point that over 50% of all supplies fell to the Viet Minh. Giap no longer needed to import artillery rounds; he simply used French supplies dropped behind his lines.

First a series of attacks were launched on the five strongpoints to the east. Hills were constantly captured and recaptured as the battle switched from side to side. Dominique, the highest strongpoint, changed hands several times. The hill, overlooking the entire valley, was too large for the French to defend with their limited manpower. Finally captured by the Viet Minh, the French managed to hold on to only a part of the position.

The key to the five hills was Eliane, especially Eliane 2. Some of the fiercest and most continuous fighting took place on

Memorial on Dominique

The Cneter of Resistance is easily seen from Dominique

this position. If this strongpoint fell, the battle would be over.

The battle of the five hills was vicious and valor and cowardice lived with both armies. When Algerians retreated in panic from Dominique, Lieutenant Brunbrouck, defying orders to withdraw, held firm with his African artillerymen and, lowering his guns, devastated the Viet Minh attack. A company of French paratroopers reinforced the southern end of Eliane 2. Just six Foreign Legion Paratroopers and a corporal remained after the Viet Minh opened up with recoilless rifles and machineguns. Soon they were gone. Only a few Moroccans remained to hold the position at the crest where the Governor's house once stood. Bigeard saved the position by launching a counter-attack by Lieutenant Lucciana and his paratroopers and Lieutenant Fournier and a force of the 1st Foreign Legion paratroopers supported by two tanks.

According to historian Bernard Fall, almost 4,000 French colonial soldiers deserted. With no place to go, they dug into the banks of the Nam Yum and lived by stealing food from the fighting troops. De Castries considered having them arrested or killed, but continued to leave them alone. They became known as the "Rats of the Nam Yum."

During the battle the French did not sit back and take a beating. Almost daily they launched their own attacks against the Viet Minh. Major Bigeard led most of these attacks. In an operation around Ban Ong Pet, his force killed over 350 Viet Minh and sent the rest fleeing leaving behind five anti-aircraft guns, twelve .50 caliber machine guns, two bazookas, fourteen automatic rifles, and hundreds of other weapons.

Not everything was going Giap's way. Because of his tremendous losses, many of his troops started to revolt. They felt their lives were being lost due to poor tactics and uncreative thinking. General Giap stopped many frontal attacks and had coolies dig more approach trenches to help save lives. He also gave the troops occasional rest periods between attacks while still maintaining his artillery bombardment 24 hours a day. He was also short of doctors. The Viet Minh had only one surgeon, and several poorly trained general practitioners, for all their wounded.

Dr. Grauwin operates in hospital

French medical conditions were a disaster. The main hospital was designed for 44 patients. They now had 800. Wounded were piled upon one another, stacked in every corner, and lined the halls. Many sat outside. To add to the problems the rainy season had started. The Valley of Dien Bien Phu receives more rain than any other part of Vietnam. Trenches, including the hospital, filled with water. Medical supplies were short and wounds crawled with maggots as the floors filled with sewage. The dead could no longer be buried in the cemetery and were now buried where they fell, or left to rot when they could not be retrieved.

Wounded are stacked everywhere

French artillery was in terrible shape. Because of the open positions, guns and men were rapidly being destroyed. Ammunition was scarce. By March 31st they were down to half their effectiveness and had suffered 85 casualties. They soon had more guns than crews. In defense of the five hills they had fired over 13,000 rounds in a single night. Just as they were getting desperate and felt they could not hold out much longer, Giap stopped his attacks.

Since all of the five hills proved too costly to take, Giap held what he could and next attacked the western fortifications. Two Viet

Minh battalions attacked a small force of Lieutenant Spozio's Legionnaires, T'ai', and Vietnamese in strongpoint Hugette 7. Three tanks, commanded by Sergeant Boussrez, and about 100 mixed troops launched a counter attack. Shocked by the counter-attack, the Viet Minh retreated. Seriously wounded, Lieutenant Spozio had been holding out against the two Viet Minh battalions with just thirteen men. But saving Hugette 7 was for nothing. Colonel Langlais ordered the strongpoint abandoned.

Fighting on Eliane 2 had not ceased, however. Part of the position was still held by the Viet Minh. Langlais ordered an attack by a unit of the 1st Foreign Legion Parachute Battalion to drive them off. After a fierce fight most of the position was back in French hands, but their commander, Major Guiraud, was wounded.

For several days, French artillery was ineffective. Only eight guns remained operable at Dien Bien Phu and four at Isabelle, a strongpoint five miles to the south who were completely cut off and fighting their own war. New parts to repair the guns, and new artillerymen, needed to be parachuted in. Reinforcements were being miss-dropped straight into Viet Minh lines and immediately captured or killed. The two fresh water tanks were destroyed so soldiers came down with various intestinal diseases from drinking local water.

Giap attacked Hugette 6 at the end of the airstrip. Again tanks drove them off. Fighting continued on Eliane 2 but the Viet Minh were worn down and the few remaining forces finally retreated leaving behind 1,500 dead rotting on the hillsides with 300 dead French.

Commander Le Trong Tan ordered Colonel Thuy's 165th Infantry Regiment to attack Hugette 6. Supported by the 401st Heavy Weapons Company, four battalions attacked Lieutenants, Rastouil and Francois, and eighty-eight Legionnaires. Captain Cledic, who had arrived only the day before, launched a counter-attack from Elaine 2, ran the entire distance across the airstrip from one end of the battlefield to the other, and charged directly into the southern flank of the Viet Minh. Supported by two tanks, Conti and Ettlingen, Cledic's force routed the Viets and saved the remaining twenty Legionnaires of Hugette 6. Within the trenches lay 500 dead Viet Minh. Another 300 were sprawled in the barbed wire. The French had lost 200.

Giap sent for reinforcements from his reserve pool of 25,000. He also radioed

More Viet Minh guns arrive

China to send more anti-aircraft guns and he gave his men a short break as they regrouped.

Ten American Chaffee tanks had been dropped in pieces into the Valley before the siege began. Legionnaires, using makeshift hoists, had assembled them by hand. Only four remained operable at Dien Bien Phu, another two at Isabelle. The Viet Minh were knocking out the American 105's as quickly as they could be repaired. Shrapnel easily tore open the recoil mechanisms. Six pieces were rendered inoperable in a single night during the fight for Hugette 6. Two replacement 75mm recoilless guns were dropped behind Viet Minh lines. Major Bigeard launched an attack to Ban Co My, a mile-and-a-half away, and recovered them both along with a refrigerated container containing blood.

On April 13 another surgical team, under the direction of Captain Hantz, was parachuted in. Casualties had mounted tremendously and soldiers were treating many wounded on the hillsides. There was simply no room in the hospitals. The first cases of gangrene broke out due to lack of medicines. The Viet Minh suddenly sent a tremendous bombardment into the Center of Resistance. Lieutenant Brunbrouck, who had saved Dominique, was killed. His last words were, "Keep firing; we've got to show them." Viet Minh commandos cut the airstrip in half isolating Hugette 6.

Tanks continue to be knocked out

Because some reinforcements had been successfully dropped, French fighting forces increased to almost 5,000. Many of these would soon be destroyed and by the last days of the siege only a little over 3,000 remained. Giap still had 35,000 plus an additional 12,000 artillerymen and engineers. He wanted more and sent for Battalions 910 and 920 of Mountaineer Regiment 148 from Laos, and battalion 970 and 900. He felt he had the French beaten and he was taking no chances.

Three platoon commanders, Lieutenants Rastouil, Francois, and Meric, gathered in a trench in Hugette 6 to discuss their almost hopeless situation with Captain Bizard. A shell landed in their midst killing Rastouil and seriously wounding Meric. They were also out of water and an attempt to dig a well failed. With so much water falling all around there was none to drink. Almost 200 soldiers now held the position and each one needed a half-gallon of water a day to survive the heat.

The duty of supplying Hugette 6 with water and ammunition fell to the Viet Minh prisoners of war, called PIM's. Because they could not be transported out, they were put to work. In charge were Lieutenant Patrico and Major Clemencon. The PIM's seemed devoted to them and almost none attempted to escape. In fact, at the end of the battle the Viet Minh wanted to kill the men in charge of the prisoners. Not a single PIM would point them out and when Major Clemencom was taken away, hands tied behind his back, many prisoners stood and saluted him. Over 50% of the PIM's died in the Valley.

In Mid April a French force, with 40 PIM's carrying supplies, fought their way to Hugette 6. They suffered heavy casualties and had to be rescued by a counter-attack in order to return. On a positive note the Valley received their biggest airdrop so far giving them several days rations and shells to continue the fight. Colonel de Castries was promoted to brigadier general. His stars, and a complimentary bottle of champagne, fell behind Viet Minh lines.

The decision to abandon Hugette 6 was made after another attempt to send supplies failed. The Viet Minh had tightly sealed off the position. Not even a rescue unit could get

French wounded are treated in the open. Giap's idea of clogging the camp with casualties worked

through so Captain Bizard was informed he could surrender. He refused and informed de Castries that they would break out. The Viet Minh constantly preferred taking French prisoners as opposed to killing them and even during some of the fiercest fighting, with bullets flying everywhere, asked them to surrender.

Bizard had his remaining men tied sandbags around their necks to hang over their chests like flack jackets. Early in the morning, under the cover of fog, they charged through Giap's surprised lines and rushed for the Center of Resistance. Few made it through, but Captain Bizard was one of them. The defense of Hugette 6 had cost the French 106 killed, 49 wounded, and 79 missing. Only five of sixteen officers survived.

With the position fallen, the Viet Minh moved new anti-aircraft guns to the end of the airstrip. Giap was slowly suffocating Dien Bien Phu and French drop zones became smaller and smaller causing more supplies to fall to the enemy. Only two 155's still worked and two more of the 105's were damaged. Giap turned his forces to Hugette 1, on the northwest. He was determined to take one position at a time until all were overcome. Chinese advisors, wearing a small insignia showing the sun, had also been assigned to most of the 37mm anti-aircraft guns.

Hugette 1 suffered the same difficulties as Hugette 6: isolated, no water, and almost impossible to supply. The Viet Minh overran the position. The French launched a failed attack to retake the strongpoint totally decimating their last reserves. Most of their vehicles were also inoperable meaning they could no longer gather and haul supplies except by manpower.

A small French memorial and cemetery sits just south of de Castries bunker

The French still remained aggressive and launched several attacks on, and around, the five hills often surprising the Viet Minh who felt they were finished as an offensive force. Accidents often happen in war and now one occurred with a miss-guided bombing mission. Many civilians, mostly women and children, had been gathered in the village of Noong Nhai between the Center of Resistance and Isabelle. Most history books fail to mention this unfortunate incident, but on April 24th many civilians were killed when bombs fell from the overhead B-26s.

Dien Bien Phu was almost finished. Generals Navarre and Cogny were no longer talking and had almost forgotten the battle as they attempted to blame each other for the fiasco. They tried to place some of the blame on the United States, who had approved the operation and saying they had cut the supply lines in Korea through bombing and that the French could do the same. The Viet Minh would strangle without supplies. It was a lie, of course. The U.S. Air Force had not cut a single supply line in Korea. The U.S. had agreed to intervene if the French got into trouble. They were in trouble now.

Meetings were held in Washington to find a solution. The idea of mass bombings was discussed, but they had a quicker solution – atomic bombs. American commanders decided that dropping several atomic bombs would devastate the Viet Minh and clear the area. The effect on the French troops seemed to not be an issue. They sent the proposal to the president. Eisenhower agreed but only on the condition that the British also agreed. The British discounted such a disastrous and ridiculous solution and because of their humane and rational decision, no bombs were dropped. The U. S. readied 98 B-29 Superfortress bombers and 450 fighter jets to intervene, but they were never used. The French were on their own.

Photo by Nev Tickner

Memorial at Noong Nhai

The French high command equivocated about support not knowing if they should continue the defense of Dien Bien Phu, or let it fall. Only 4% of French forces were there, an acceptable loss for any military. What they could not handle was the loss to French pride. As a result they sometimes dribbled in meager amounts of supplies, and sometimes not. They constantly assured de Castries he would have full support, even after they decided to let the post fall. As a result, the soldiers continued to fight thinking relief was on the way.

On April 27th the Viet Minh had pushed their roads to the Valley so supplies did not have to be hand carried from Tuan Giao. Massive amounts poured to the troops. They made an easy target, but the French had only a single 155 still operable and the barrel was so shot-out that shells traveled just several hundred yards before rolling to the ground. The few remaining 105's had to conserve their ammunition for the next attack.

Giap employed new efforts to protect his troops. The troops had been shelled as they dug their approach trenches. For added safety, coolies carried logs from the hills and built protective roofs over the trenches.

With just a week left before the fall, the French continued to launce forays into Viet Minh lines, killing soldiers, destroying equipment, and taking prisoners. But disaster struck again. A food depot was hit, as was an artillery ammuni-

Tank and debris sit near the site of the hospital

tion depot. Over 600 precious 105 shells blew up making the situation in the Valley even more desperate. Only one tank, "Auerstaest" remained after "Dauaumont" sustained a direct hit wounding the entire crew.

The Legionnaires, especially, found reasons to fight. When two cases of "Vinogel," a wine concentrate, fell behind enemy lines they launched an attack from Eliane 2 to retrieve the precious liquid. During the raid they destroyed a blockhouse, damaged two others, killed ten Viet Minh and wounded many others, and suffered no casualties of their own.

It was time to finish the job and Giap launched his final attacks. Positions started to fall. De Castries radioed Hanoi, "No more reserves left. Fatigue and wear and tear on the units terrible."

In the west, Hugettes 1, 2, and 3 came under diversionary attacks. The 308th People's Army Division rushed toward Hugette 5, defended by just Lieutenant de Stabenrath and 29 men. The position fell quickly. In the east Elaine 1 and Dominique 3 fell. The Viet Minh concentrated on Elaine 2, the key to the battle. Viet Minh and Legionnaires battled hand-to-hand. The position held. The Viet Minh started to dig a tunnel under the position in an effort to stack it with explosives and blow up the command post.

Because the French had less than 3,000 combat troops, any wounded that could walk were asked to leave the hospitals and join the various positions. Most felt they were going to die anyway and they wanted to die with their comrades. Even Captain Lucciani, badly wounded three times, returned to command Hugette 4. Orders were sent to de Castries. If Dien Bien Phu could not be held, they were not to capitulate. They were to decide upon a time to stop fighting and simply lay down their arms. No white flags were to be flown.

Command post on Elaine 2

The French were not finished yet. The men, knowing everything was hopeless, refused to quit. Several more days of fight remained in them.

The wounded Captain Lucciani, on Hugette 4 with eighty Legionnaires and Moroccans, now faced one of the largest Viet Minh attacks during the battle. Lieutenant Colonel Manh Quan and over 3,000 men, supported by a defining artillery barrage, charged the small force of Frenchmen. The French held them off for over two hours littering the field and barbed wire with dead Viets. A young Moroccan Lieutenant radioed the final message from the strongpoint saying they were down to ten men.

Even then Major Guiraud, outraged at the loss of Hugette 4, launched a counter attack with just 100 men. They managed to breach the defenses of Hugette 4 but, 100 men have no chance of defeating several thousand and they were beaten back.

The men were fighting in the trenches with mud and water up to their waists as the rains continued to fall. They still refused to quit. The Viet Minh, determined to gain their freedom at any cost, also refused to quit. French artillery reported they had only one day's supply of ammunition remaining.

Captain Pouget was sent to relieve Captain Coutant and the tired troops on Eliane 2. Coutant familiarized him with the position. Most of the fortifications were blown apart and the hillsides stank with the rotting bodies of over 1,500 Viet Minh and several hundred Moroccans and Legionnaires. He failed to mention that the Viet Minh were digging a tunnel under the position, but Captain Edeme, whose company sat directly over the shaft, knew. He heard them digging. He told Pouget and the replacements. Pouget sent a small detachment, led by Sergeant Clinele, to destroy it. Clinele and his commandos were cut down. "Bazeille," a disabled tank, sat just below the command post and was being used as a bunker to cover one of the slopes.

May 6th, 1954, the final night of fighting, saw the Viet Minh pack 3,000 pounds of TNT into their tunnel under Eliane 2. Colonel Langlais and Major Biegard, knowing the final battle was at hand, had visited each strongpoint.

The tank "Bazeilles" remains on the hillside of Eliane 2 where it was used as a bunker

They wished all the commanders and men good luck then added that regardless what ever happened, no reinforcements were available.

All the strongpoints erupted with a tremendous artillery barrage. The barrage was made even more deadly with the addition of newly arrived Katyusha rockets. The remaining medical supplies blew apart as did small

Entrance to the Viet Minh Cemetary near Elaine 2

packets of dropped ammunition and depots of all kinds. All fire suddenly moved to Eliane 2 and 4. The final attack had begun.

One thousand of Lieutenant Colonel Vu Yen's Viet Minh "Capital Regiment" rushed the eastern slope of Eliane 2. The regiment was the best in Giap's entire army. Lieutenant Robin, forward observer for Pouget and his Legionnaires, called in a deadly accurate artillery strike. Because there were so few rounds remaining, the barrage lasted just a few short minutes. When it stopped the Capital Regiment had vanished, blown to bits by the explosions.

Viet Minh graves

Claudine 5 fell. Two Regiments attacked Eliane 10 and were beaten back by 30 soldiers of French Vietnamese.

Sergeants Bruni and Ballait had crawled into the tank "Bazeilles" on Elaine 2. After the decimation of the failed Viet Minh attack, they had experienced almost three hours of respite. They knew it would not last and they prepared the 50. Cal. Machine guns with all the ammunition they could find. Farther down the line Captain Edeme's entire company blew into the air from the underground explosion. Men went flying everywhere, but the thick layer of rising earth cushioned many of them. Quickly gathering their senses, they moved machine guns to the edge of the gaping hole and waited the attack. The Viet Minh, running into the hole, could not climb out and were cut down by the Legionnaires. Viets running around the pit were herded in and killed by a counter-attack from Captain Pouget over the top of the strongpoint.

Pouget and General Giap fought with the understanding that everything depended on Eliane 2. Captain Pouget knew that if he failed to hold the position, all Dien Bien Phu was finished. He needed more men and especially more ammunition. Giap knew that if he did not take the position, all the months of death and sacrifice were for nothing. The war would continue to slog on. It was May 7th. The battle was about to end.

Only 100 rounds of mortar ammunition remained in all the camp; 300 rounds of 105; and eleven rounds of 155.

Pouget had only 35 men left for the entire defense of Eliane 2. They fought on and he radioed for reinforcements and ammunition. There were none available. He asked for permission to retreat. He was told that as a paratrooper he was there to die. He agreed and destroyed his radio.

Without ammunition, they fought with hand grenades. Around the command post the small band of brothers piled bodies as protection. Captain Pouget threw the final grenade and was knocked down by a concussion grenade from a Viet Minh soldier. They were told to remove their shoes, so they would not run away, and led off the strongpoint. But two Legionnaires refused to surrender. The last shots heard on the hillside were from Sergeants Bruni and Ballait as they continued fire from the tank.

The French at Dien Bien Phu were finally finished. Gip launched all-out attacks on every French position. One by one they started to fall. De Castries sent a message to Giap. The French would stop fighting at 1730 hours (5:30PM) on April 7th, 1954.

Vietnam had gained her freedom.

The French are marched to prisoner camps after the battle. Of the 14,000 French soldiers in the battle only about 3,000 survived the battle and the camps. The Viet Minh lose an estimated 25,000 troops.

Further Reading on the siege at Dien Bien Phu:

First a Torch - by Richard Baker
Dien Bien Phu - by General Giap
Hell in a Very Small Place - by Bernard Fall
The Battle of Dien Bien Phu - by Jules Roy
Valley of Death - by Ted Morgan
Dien Bien Phu - by Howard Simpson

Made in the USA
Lexington, KY
19 April 2013